Super Mums
FROM ME TO YOU

Edited by Emily Johnstone

First published in Great Britain in 2017 by:

 Young**Writers**

Young Writers
Remus House
Coltsfoot Drive
Peterborough
PE2 9BF
Telephone: 01733 890066
Website: www.youngwriters.co.uk

Printed and bound in the UK by BookPrintingUK
Website: www.bookprintinguk.com

FOREWORD

Here at Young Writers our defining aim is to promote the joys of reading and writing to children and young adults and we are committed to nurturing the creative talents of the next generation. By allowing them to see their own work in print we believe their confidence and love of creative writing will grow.

We are proud to present this collection of poems, the result of our latest competition 'Super Mums'. Using poetry as a tool to express their appreciation and admiration of all these things a mother does, these young writers give personal dedications to the irreplaceable super mum in their life. The selection process was a very difficult task, yet the love and enthusiasm put into all of the entries ensured that we enjoyed reading each and every one.

Including a medley of different voices and poetic styles, such as rhyming verse and the acrostic, this is an endearing anthology in which talented young writers use their creative flow of words to give an important message to their mum in a million: thank you.

Emily Johnstone

CONTENTS

THE POEMS

CONGRATULATIONS
ETHAN-RAUL, YOU ARE OUR WINNING POET
FROM THE SUPER MUMS COMPETITION!

WHAT IS A MUM?

What is a Mum?
A weaner and musher, a milky tooth brusher
A rocker and feeder, a storytime reader
A fairy cake baker and fancy dress maker
A wiper and washer and bad habit squasher
A dirty sheet changer, a room re-arranger
A keen stain remover, a wielder of Hoover
A peeler and cooker, appointment booker
A loyal defender and Christmas card sender
A playdate arranger, alerter of danger
A suitcase packer, a dishwasher stacker
A 'be quiet' hisser, a cuddly kisser
An early riser, a birthday surpriser
A list compiler, a proud parent smiler
A talented wrapper, a tireless clapper
A lavatory flusher, a praiser and gusher
A listening ear, a good referee-r
A source of a fiver, a free taxi driver
A smoothie blender and broken heart mender
A consummate shopper, embarrassing bopper
A grocery bagger and homework nagger
That's what makes a mum!

Ethan-Raul Patel

1

MY MUM

My mum is great, caring and kind,
Clever as a calculator, she has an extraordinary mind.
Best friends forever, that's my mum and me,
Forever and always, you see.
My mum stands out among all the rest
And the reason for that is that she is simply the best.

My mum works hard, night and day,
But always has time to have fun and play.
My mum always works as hard as she can
And if anything goes wrong, she always has a plan.
My mum works so hard and always tries her best
And this is why she stands out from the rest.

Life with my mum is happy and bright,
She is always there, like a reassuring light.
All my siblings, my brothers, sister and me
Are all so proud to call her our mummy.
You see, my mum stands out from all the rest
And the reason for that is because she is simply the best.

In my heart holds many memories, of all the loving things
she's done
And I really do hope she knows, that I am thankful for each
one.
My mum works so hard and always tries her best
And this is why she is better than all the rest.

You see, ever since I remember,
I remember loving her.
My mum is so special, she is the best

And this is why she stands out from all the rest.
Now Mum, I just want to say,
'I love you Mum, happy Mother's Day!'

Amelia Smythe

Alton Convent School, Alton

MUM

Mum, it's hard to find the words to say
How much you mean to me.
But if it wasn't for your love and care
I don't know where I'd be.

How do you do it all, Mum?
Be a chauffeur, cook and friend,
Yet find time to be a playmate,
I just can't comprehend.

You always overlook my faults
And see the best in me,
You always say to me to be
The very best that you can be.

Nobody's quite like you, Mum,
With you in my life, I'm blessed,
I love you so much, and I want you to know
I think you're the very best Mum.

Isabelle Clarke
Alton Convent School, Alton

THANK YOU MUM

Dear Mum I want to say,
Thank you for each and every day,
She takes me to school, never late,
Looking as glamorous as Princess Kate.

She makes me dinner which is so yummy,
Thank you so much my fabulous mummy.
She helps me with homework if it is hard
And spends her money on me from her credit card.

She watches my matches even in rain,
She probably finds it a right old pain.
So thank you Mum, I really mean it,
I love you so much, every single bit.

Erin D'Arcy (10)

Alton Convent School, Alton

MUM

You're the sunshine that lights up my day,
You are like a god to me,
Over the years you have seen me angry,
Happy, smiling and wiped my tears away.

You are the one who gives me guidance,
You are the one who loves me,
You are my life and soul
And without you, I wouldn't be.

You are as pretty as autumn,
As happy as spring,
As warm as the summer
And you sparkle like the winter.

If you were not here to care for me,
I don't know where I would be.
Your unconditional love,
I will never forget.

You're the sunshine that lights up my day,
You are like a god to me,
Mums are a promise from God that you
Will have a friend forever!

Mia Passingham

Alton Convent School, Alton

MOM

First touch from you... how warm,
First sound from you can stop my cry.

Mom was the first word I could say,
Mom means everything to me.

Sometimes you say... I close my ears,
Whatever I say... you want to hear.

You protected me like an egg in the storm,
You may be tired from anything,
But never be tired to do anything for me.

Miracle of true love... nothing to compare,
My wonder mom.

Alia Waiyasil
Arnhem Wharf Primary School, London

MY ADORABLE MOTHER

I will love you forever
And forever you will be
The most wonderful mother.
You mean everything to me.

I thought of buying you flowers
In the usual way
But I knew you would prefer
A forever bouquet!

Your arms were always open
When I needed a warm hug
Your heart knew
When I needed a friend
Your gentle eyes told
Me if I did things wrong
Your love gave me joy
And happiness to my heart.

A mother who always cares,
A mother who's always there.
A mother who always prays,
A mother who always stays.
When things get rough,
When life gets tough,
When all is just too much to bear,
God's words she always shares.

Like a nurse, you look after me.
Like a teacher, you teach me to learn.
Like a lifeguard, you teach me to swim.

Like a superhero, you save the day.
Like a map, you help me find my way.
Like a tissue, you dry out my tears.
Like home, you are where my heart is.

Charlene Contreras

Arnhem Wharf Primary School, London

UNTITLED

Moms, moms they give you chores,
Moms, moms they help your sores,
Moms, moms they're nice to meet,
Moms, moms they're nice and sweet.

It's easy to show love on Mother's Day.

Moms, moms loving you,
Moms, moms helping with the things you do.

They care about you,
But do you too? On the special day
Mother's Day.

Antony Terence Armett

Fairfield Endowed CE Junior School, Buxton

MY FANTASTIC MUM

M y mum is better than the rest
Y ou smell as sweet as a rose blooming

F orever I will love my mum
A bit of love is worth it
N o one is better than you
T ears will never appear
A wesome mum every day
S adness runs away like raindrops
T he love will always shine brightly
I love you to the end of the moon
C aring for me always

M y mum is best at making pancakes
U nder the stars you shine brightly
M ost wonderful Mum.

Alfie-Lee Worthington

King's Court First School, Windsor

MY MUMMY

M y mum helps me with everything
U means usually never cross with me
M e and Frankie love her so much
M illions of hugs you give to me
Y ou are the best there is.

Zack Guarnieri
King's Court First School, Windsor

My Mother

M y mum's excellent
Y ou're better than everyone

M y mum knows everything
O h! Days with Mum are the best
T ennis is my mum's favourite sport
H ere and there she's always there
E very day she loves me
R est, Mum, because you deserve it.

Elliot Jack Whitehorn

King's Court First School, Windsor

My Mum

My mum is like a pillow,
My mum has hair like gold,
My mum takes care of me so much,
My mum is the best in the world.

My mum is like a rainbow,
My mum is Super Mum,
My mum will always be so special to me.
Thank you Mum for everything you do!

Heidi Nicole Green

King's Court First School, Windsor

SUPER MUM

My mum is as clever as ever.
My mum is the best cook.
My mum gives the best hugs.
My mum is really fun.
My mum is as beautiful as gold.
My mum is out of this world.
My mum is as gentle as a feather.
My mum is as cuddly as a soft toy.

Harrison Barr

King's Court First School, Windsor

SUPER MUM

M y mum loves me as much as she hugs me
O h the memories you give me
T hough you tell me off I know you still love me
H earts love you especially Dad, Eloise, me and Kiana
E yes that sparkle like diamonds
R ight and bright always.

I love you, Mother, altogether,
You mean the world to me!

Ben Doncaster

King's Court First School, Windsor

MOTHER

M is for how marvellous she is.
O is for all the old memories she gives me.
T is for her three children.
H is for how she helps me with my homework.
E very moment is special with her around.
R is for everything she remembers.

M-O-T-H-E-R spells the word Mother,
A word that means everything to me!
No Mother could be more special than her!

Madeleine Lewis

King's Court First School, Windsor

SUPER MUM

My mum is amazing,
I love her very much,
I wish I could tell her how very, very much.
Her hair as brown as chocolate,
Her eyes as blue as the sky,
Her voice is like an angel,
She is as kind as the queen,
She is always trying to make me happy,
She is as beautiful as a butterfly,
Her teeth as white as snow.
Her clothes are as pretty as a flower,
My mum means the world to me.

Emma Dyson
King's Court First School, Windsor

MOTHER'S DAY

M um, I'll love you to the day you die

O ther mums are not like you

T here I see in you a heart of pure gold

H ope you have a good Mother's Day

E very day you work to earn money for us

R oses smell just like you

S ometimes you make me feel like I'm special to you

D ay after day you work hard to make us survive for the winter

A lways you make me shine in your eyes

Y ou make me happy every day like a star.

Oskar Edward Thompson Totten

King's Court First School, Windsor

My Super Foster Mum

M y foster mum is the kindest
Y ou're the one in my heart

S he is the best
U p above the rest
P erfect like a rose
E very day you make my day shine
R oses are your favourite flower

M y magical foster mum
U nusual and nice to me
M y foster mum is lovely!

Happy Mother's Day to every mum in the world.

Reid Cummings
King's Court First School, Windsor

My super foster mum

MY MUM

M y mum is the best
O nly you can be the best
T ears wiped from my eyes
H er cuddles keep me safe
E very day she works hard
R eally loves you lots
S he makes me happy

D oesn't laugh at me
A lways makes lovely pancakes
Y ou smell beautiful.

Redmond Edward Barron-Cheeseman
King's Court First School, Windsor

SUPER MUM

My mum is as quiet as a floating feather.
My mum is as clever as a teacher.
My mum is as happy as a child.
My mum is as funny as a clown.

Her hair is like chocolate.
Her eyes sparkle like glitter.
Her mouth is as red as rosebuds.
I love my mum and she loves me too!

Charlotte Grace Cahill
King's Court First School, Windsor

MY MUM IS EPIC

M y mum is the best
Y ou're better than the rest

M y mum helps me do my homework
U nique stuff she does
M y mum is epic

I love my mum so much
S he is the best

E very day she is there for me
P erfect mums are the best
I love her so much
C elebrate Mother's Day.

Harry Fountain

King's Court First School, Windsor

SUPER MUM

M y mum is the best in the world!
U nderstanding me always!
M akes me very happy when I'm sad!
M eans so much to me and my family!
Y ou are the most wonderful mum ever!

Ryan Field
King's Court First School, Windsor

MY FANTASTIC MUM

M y mum is the best, she is better than the rest
Y ou are the favourite mum in the world

F or you, I hope you like my poem
A wesome mums have magic powers
N ice mums help you tidy up
T ake me back home please, I have a present for you
A ll the love you give me is sweet and warm
S uper mums help you tidy up, she is also like a sweet rose
T ake the chocolates and eat them up
I like you because you always help me with homework
C an you always stay by my side?

M y mum always smells nice like roses
U s and you are sweet like cherries
M ums are the best, they buy chocolate and all the rest.

Layla-Mai Blackwell

King's Court First School, Windsor

SUPER MUM

My mum is as pretty as a daisy.
My mum is not lazy.
My mum has kind thoughts in her head.
My mum is never in bed.
My mum is clever.
My mum is dumb never.
My mum is not old.
My mum is always cold.
My mum is funny.
My mum is not a bunny.
My mum is very fast.
My mum could not cook in the past.
My mum has lots of luck.
My mum hates lots of muck.

Arjun Chakrabarti

King's Court First School, Windsor

Super Mum

My mum is so helpful,
Like I'm paper, she's glue
And whenever I'm feeling down
She always gets me some shoes!

My mum is a multitasker,
She looks after us all,
Me, my dog, my brother, my sister,
We all give her a call!

I love her so dearly,
She is the best Mum ever,
She loves her sewing as well as me,
With her needle and leather.

My mum is the best,
She's like a superhero
And I'm telling you she never is
Ever, ever zero!

Josie Clarke

King's Court First School, Windsor

SUPER MUM

S uper mums are the best
U nique mums are worth it
P erfect mums are cool because they help with my tests
E verywhere my mum is there
R esting for your mum is nice

M y mum is better than the rest
U se her when you need help
M ums know better!

William Thomas
King's Court First School, Windsor

28

SUPER MUM

My mum is kind, the best you can find.
My mum is beautiful like a butterfly.
My mum is helpful like an angel.
My mum is always such fun.

My mum is wonderful.
My mum is always fun to be with.
My mum sparkles like the stars in the sky.
My mum is the best there can be.

Ethan James Tomaselli

King's Court First School, Windsor

29

SUPER MUM

My mum is as kind as anyone.
My mum helps me with my homework.
My mum gives me lots of hugs which I love.
My mum is the best!

Arthur Joseph Henry Shutler
King's Court First School, Windsor

Mummy

M ummy is lovely
U sually helps with my homework
M ummy is beautiful like a pot of flowers
M ummy gives me lots of hugs
Y ou are wonderful.

Shannon Kaya

Lanesend Primary School, Isle Of Wight

My Mum

My mum helps me with baking.
My mum loves me.
My mummy plays with me.
My mummy helps tidy.
My mummy tucks me in bed.
My mum hugs me.
My mum makes my food.

Grace Beasley

Lanesend Primary School, Isle Of Wight

Mummy

My mummy's like a
Kind helper,
Hotel stayer,
Busy worker,
Sand builder,
Packed lunch maker,
Busy shopper,
Best cuddler.

Freya Smith
Lanesend Primary School, Isle Of Wight

MY LOVELY MUM

My mum is beautiful and kind.
She helps me tidy my room.
My mum is lovely and pretty.
She looks like a pretty girl.
I love you, Mum.

Kaitlin Gemma Kelly

Lanesend Primary School, Isle Of Wight

MUMMY

M y mummy is like a dream
U nderstanding, beautiful mother
M y mummy is so nice
M y mummy has a soft voice like a rainbow
Y ou are the best.

Scarlett Thomas

Lanesend Primary School, Isle Of Wight

MY MUMMY

Kind helper
Sea paddler
Good summer
Packed luncher
Wine drinker
Best kisser.

Cloe Mcdonough (7)

Lanesend Primary School, Isle Of Wight

36

MOTHER

M um is interested a lot
O ther people like her a lot
T rains a lot
H elps me a lot
E very day she loves me a lot
R eads to me a lot.

Sophie Buggs

Lanesend Primary School, Isle Of Wight

My Mum

She is beautiful, pretty and wonderful.
Amazing Mum, an epic Mum
And funny Mum.
Fun maker.
Super Mum, great Mum.
Wonderful Mum.

Poppy Thomas

Lanesend Primary School, Isle Of Wight

UNTITLED

She's healthy,
Beautiful and pretty.
She's the most caring girl ever.
She is like a superhero.

Alfie Hough

Lanesend Primary School, Isle Of Wight

LOVELY MUM

Lovely Mum
Funny Mum
Amazing Mum
Wonderful Mum.

Jack Welsman
Lanesend Primary School, Isle Of Wight

MY MUM

My mum smells of the shower.
The trees in the shade of the sun.
My mum is a beauty to my heart.

Olivia Cockburn

Lanesend Primary School, Isle Of Wight

MY LOVELY MUM

I feel like I love my mum.
She helps me with my maths
And is beautiful, pretty and lovely.

Henry Wyld
Lanesend Primary School, Isle Of Wight

FROM MASON

My mum helps me with my homework
And helps me cook.
I love that she is funny.
She is smart, fun, fantastic
And she gives me gifts.

Mason Miller

Lanesend Primary School, Isle Of Wight

LOVE MUM

My mum loves me, me, me.
She cares about me, me, me.
My mum thinks I smell nice.
Night-night, sleep tight.

Ava Munt

Lanesend Primary School, Isle Of Wight

UNTITLED

My mum is pretty like a butterfly.
My mum is patient in a line.
My mum is caring to people like me.
My mum is a princess.
My mum is kind-hearted.
My mum is a saint.
My mum is smart and beautiful.
My mum is a butterfly.

Lorenna Southon

Lanesend Primary School, Isle Of Wight

MY MUMMY

My mum hugs me.
Does dinner for me.
Does my laces for me.
My mummy helps me.
My mummy plays with me.
I love my mummy.

Jack Rawe (7)

Lanesend Primary School, Isle Of Wight

MOTHER

M y mummy likes me
O h every day we love each other
T he times we play
H elps me with everything
E verything we do together is great
R eal love!

Faith Olivia Rimmer

Lanesend Primary School, Isle Of Wight

MUMMY

M y mum is super at making me laugh
U sually cheeky but not always
M um is so much like the best
M ummy is awesome
Y ou are the loveliest mum ever.

Kira Early

Lanesend Primary School, Isle Of Wight

Untitled

Loving, funny, Mum is.
The best mum in the world today.
Mum is fantastic today.
Lovely Mum is good today.
My lovely mum.

Alfie Lee Brett
Lanesend Primary School, Isle Of Wight

My Beautiful Mummy

My mummy is a beautiful creature and fantastic.
She always cares about me
And puts presents down
When it is my birthday and Christmas.
She loves me forever and ever.

George James Knight
Lanesend Primary School, Isle Of Wight

SUPER MUM

Her worn-out tired feet
As busy as bees
Rushing around the house
Her millions of multicoloured handbags
Hanging off her arms
Sweet-smelling perfume
Wafting around the house
Aching stiff back giving her grief all day.

When she eats Mum-Vite... *Pow!*
She's Super Mum!

Her shiny jet-black hair gleaming in the sunlight
Twinkling eyes scanning the crowd for criminals
Muscular hands placed firmly on her lips
With her bright red jetpack boots
She zooms to Africa
To help orphaned children.

Back home in time to make my tea!

Rosie Kendall (11)
Lewknor CE Primary School, Watlington

SUPER MUM

The red Liverpool jacket
Actually Dad's
Slung on the stairs
The tired eyes
Are up about 5 - gaze round the room
She picks up the jacket
Put on her trainers
With no backs
The only person bothered
To walk the dogs
Strolls out the door
To go to work.

Suddenly she sees a flash
From her bracelet then dashes
to S T A R labs
Returning in her red suit
A lightning symbol on the chest
Small mask across her eyes
Bow 'n' arrow case along her back
'I've got the need for speed.'

Running the 40ish miles again
To Central City
Where there's Captain Cold
And Heatwave
Terrorising civilians of Central City
On their way to the museum
So they can steal an emerald
A diamond
Or other priceless materials
Freezing, burning everyone in sight
Two flashes of lightning
(One blue, one yellow)

It's Zoom and Reverse Flash
Super Mum runs towards Reverse Flash
He dodges and trips her
His hand vibrates
He's glaring into her soul
Lowering his hand
Moving towards her chest
But she moves with her
Speedster powers
Moves out of the way
The Man in the Yellow Suit
Tugging out her bow
Holding back the string
Firing her rope arrow
Tying him up.

Next Zoom
The Demon Speedster
Aka Hunter Solomon
Running round Super Mum
Cutting off flow of air
To her lungs
Though she manages
To time the escape right
Again she brings out her
Bow 'n' arrow
And ties him to a lamp post.

Strolling towards the museum
Memories of Harrison Wells
Flash through her mind
Before they found out about
His secret
Of being Reverse Flash
And him being
From the future

Finding out he's not Harrison Wells
But Eobart Thawne.

She started running
She slipped
On ice placed by
Leonard Snart
She recovered quickly
Captain Cold and Heatwave
Were coming out at that time
Smart went down to mock her
As Heatwave pointed his gun
She sped out and grabbed
The jewels and the two of them
To the CCPD.

Dom Thomas Evans

Lewknor CE Primary School, Watlington

SUPER MUM

Worn out feet
From walking
Thousands of steps
Her favourite perfume
I think it stinks
She talks a lot
I just ignore her
Works 24/7 looking after me
Cosmetics caked on her face
Looks after me
When I am under the weather.

She turns around and *pow*
Super Mum!
Hands on hips
Long hair
Ready to bust crime
She solves:
Me feeling ill
No beer for dad
No food for dinner
A flick of her hair
She teleports to my bedside
To give me medicine
A stomp of her foot
She's at the shop.

Thanks Mum, you're super!

Annie Hunt

Lewknor CE Primary School, Watlington

SUPER MUM...

Her favourite perfume,
I think stinks!
Detests getting dressed,
Loves her PJs,
Mummy talks a lot,
I just ignore her,
Mummy works 24/7
Looking after me.

She shakes her hair and *bang!*
She turns to Super Mum!
Her long brown hair
Flicks out of her hair band.
She is stood in the dark light
With her hand on her hip
Like she is the boss!

Solves the crisis
Of no food in the Ashby household
By flying to Aldi
Using her mighty trolley
She flew down the aisles as fast as lightning.

Tossing people to one side,
Sweeping food from the shelf,
The trolley soon filled.
Four happy children
Are relieved to see
There is now food for them all to eat.

Thank you Super Mum for
Everything you do for me.

I love you!

Elodie Ashby

Lewknor CE Primary School, Watlington

SUPER WOMAN

Multicoloured, creative clothes on her tired body
Oh come on, Mum, why do you have to
Normal,
Stressy,
Lost rose gold iPhone,
Modern, sweet-smelling perfume.

When she runs into a hyper-run
Which takes her up to speeds of 100mph
Boom! Boltwoman is here!

Glamorous she is with her sparkling white teeth
Hair flapping in the wind
Muscular arms clenched around a pistol
And a Samurai sword.

Robbers robbing a house!
With her spring boots she soars through the air
Into the mansion.

Blocking the robbers,
Guns to their heads.
'Drop everything you stole,
I'm calling the police.'
Robbers safely locked away
Crowd cheering
You're amazing, Mum!

Louis Bolton

Lewknor CE Primary School, Watlington

SUPER MUM!

Her radiant, vivid red lipstick worn-out,
Those jumpers concealed in paint.
Hair up in a chaotic bun.
Her new, strong perfume lingers
Homework she helped me with, perfect.

She winks and *boom!* She's a super-heroine.
Her fist in the air,
Strong and high
About to glide.
Her other hand firmly on her hip.
'My baby's in that burning building!'
'Super Mum to the rescue!'
She glides to the scene
Her cape flapping behind her.
She saved the day.
'Thank you Super Mum!'

Beatrice Harris

Lewknor CE Primary School, Watlington

SUPER MUM

She is always taking Dad's money
And spends it on trash.
Is always yapping about who was sick.
Is always nagging me to tidy my room.
She works 24/7, looks after me.
Always complains about her night-shift.
Worries about me 24/7.
She flies into the clouds and *pow!*
Super Mum!
She has hover boots that help zoom to her destination.
She helps stop robbers.
Saves babies from burning buildings.
Super Mum's here to save the day.
I love you Mummy!

Harry George Nicholson

Lewknor CE Primary School, Watlington

SUPER MUM

Her fine brunette hair that gusts in the air.
the monster Jack Russell (named Sassy) that annoys her.
The disastrous grimy boggy ball.
She always cooks delectable, scrumptious food,
even occasionally lasagne too.
The person who leaves twaddle everywhere,
I wonder who that is?
When you tap the charm (that I bought you)
twice on your Pandora bracelet you transform
into Super Mum.
You have your hands on your hips
with your twinkling cape breezing in the air
and your lustrous belt.
You help me with my homework,
but when you see fractions you give up.
You grab your hoverboard
and go save some people.
You save people who are falling down
a mountain in a car.
You also stop a train from falling down a canyon
and stop it in time and construct the train back.
People say, 'You're my hero Super Mum!'
You soon return and transform back
and carry on with your normal life.

Katie Wanstall

Lewknor CE Primary School, Watlington

SUPER MUM

Her lengthy colourful scarves
Swaying behind her
Cooking left to bubble
Her fluffy indigo slippers flopping along
Sweet-smelling perfume wafting through the air.

She changes her scarf, *pow!*
Super Mum!

Her prolonged legs standing still
Long blonde hair waving elegantly
Her crimson cape flowing behind her.

She's using her electrified scarf
To help give bigger, tighter hugs!
Always warm...

Thanks Super Mum
Always saving the day!

Amelia Lawley

Lewknor CE Primary School, Watlington

MOTHER'S DAY POEM

Her over-large Mrs Ashby-Fringe
could be seen from over a mile away.
The beautiful African picture that she sold on eBay
was worth more than a fiver.
That fat young bulldog that she loved so much,
was being way over fed.
Those wine stains all over the settee
which my dad gets angry about...
I wonder who put them there...
Question of the day!
Five minutes late for work
and you're still doing my make-up.
'Yes, I've got spare time,'
which generally means time to watch Total Divas.
'Flynn, we're middle-class, you're not allowed
to take your lunch in a carrier bag.'
Middle-class... more like completely swanky!
With a spin of her harlequin helicopter hair
she suddenly transforms into the
Ultimate Non-Stress super Momma.
She flips with her Catanas in hand, knees,
looks forward and shows off her seductive biceps and
hisses,
'Mmmm... tempting!'
In the process of trying to stop Doctor Evil igniting
his laser to destroy Washington DC she hustles
into the elevator and flips into Dr Evil's hideout.
As his henchmen fall to her feet,
she narrows her eyes on Dr Evil

and telepathically makes him fall to his knees,
gripping his skull as he face-plants the floor.
Those blonde streaks in her hair look
like they've been bleached.

Flynn McFadyen (10)
Lewknor CE Primary School, Watlington

SUPER MOM

Her bedraggled morning hair
Sticking out in spikes like a Mohican.
Bright sparkling eyes:
As green as the grass on a sunlit day
Her sweet-smelling, rose perfume drifting around
Bags overloading her body
Filled with shoes and *more* bags!
Her delicate, colossal hugs
As
Calm
As
A river on a mild summer's day.

When she presses her Pandora bracelet, *pow!*
She's Super Mom!
Her flourished metal pan
Swinging round her palm;
Like an elastic band
Cowboy boots standing firmly on the ground.
Her hair glistening in the sun;
As she holds her electrified wooden spoon up high
Solving crime mysteries: catching burglars.
Her eyes glaring through the mask
Like a predator about to pounce.

Amelie Van Dijk (11)
Lewknor CE Primary School, Watlington

THE ONE AND ONLY GRANDMA POEM!

My grandma is always there
Because she cares.
On holiday you let us go in the pool
Because you are cool.

You have the best smile
Even if there is a pile
Of dirty washing.

Because you are the best
Grandma ever!

Jodie Williamson

Moulton Chapel Primary School, Spalding

GRANDMA

G randma you are amazing
R esting in bed but never lazing
A t home you always look after me
N ever at tea
D on't even say it
M ad, you are really funny when you're mad
A t home you feed the fish, yay you!

Lisa Barnes

Moulton Chapel Primary School, Spalding

To Mum

You're the best Mum on the Earth,
I love you too much to say.
You have given birth
So let's celebrate you today!
You are always there for me when I need it,
Even though you don't like coffee or tea.
I hope you enjoy this poem
Every single bit,
This poem is how much I love you!

Keira Elding

Moulton Chapel Primary School, Spalding

MUMMY

Mummy,
You make food that is yummy.
You look after me,
You make great cups of tea.
You are such a treat,
You are so sweet.

Umm,
You're the best Mum,
You love me loads,
You taught me to be safe on roads,
You are full of love,
You always help me find a glove.

Mum,
You help me when I say umm.
When you tell me a story,
It is never gory.
When you give me hugs
You never think of pugs.

Roisin Williams
Moulton Chapel Primary School, Spalding

To Mummy

You are very funny
And you are as sweet as honey,
You make me laugh
And you give nice baths.

You are kind to me
And you mean a lot to me,
You are very special,
You always do lovely tea.

You make parties for me
And it's really fun
And you like buns,
You are really lovely,
When I am unhappy
You make me happy.

Holly Nurse

Moulton Chapel Primary School, Spalding

To Mummy!

My mum is the best Mum ever,
Mum, you are so pretty,
Mummy, you are nice to me,
Mummy, I love you so much,
You are so kind to me.

You are the best Mum ever,
I will always love you
And no one will stop me.
You are so kind to me
And you are beautiful,
It is true you are beautiful,
You are so nice to me
And you're the best Mum in the world.
You are so pretty
And you are lovely.

Kai Elding (9)

Moulton Chapel Primary School, Spalding

TO MUM

I love you,
You're number one, not two,
You're so joyful
And so beautiful.

You don't know how much you mean to me,
More than 1, 2, 3,
You're so cool,
More like sub-zero.

You like a strong coffee!
Sometimes tea,
But the most important thing is
That you are my mum.

Matthew Harrington

Moulton Chapel Primary School, Spalding

HAPPY MOTHER'S DAY!

She is very kind,
She has an imaginative mind,
I love her very much,
She gives everything a loving touch.

If you ever forget how much you mean to me,
I would sail all the seven seas,
You have a golden heart,
She's as sweet as a tart.

You've always supported me,
But you always love a cup of tea,
I love you
And that is true!

Jack Haunch

Moulton Chapel Primary School, Spalding

MOTHER'S DAY POEM

To Mummy,
Your food is great,
You're never late,
I love you
And you love me too!

Mum, you're so kind,
Always with me in mind,
You love good coffee
And you probably like toffee!

You are very funny,
You give me pocket money,
Mum, you are very sweet,
You are such a treat.

Happy Mother's Day!

Niamh Williams

Moulton Chapel Primary School, Spalding

WHAT DOES A MUM MEAN?

My mum is brave and she is nice and kind.
My mum is so loving and blows my mind.

My mum is happy and cool.
My mum is hugging, funny and cool
Because she goes in the pool.

Maddox Mulligan

St Elizabeth's RC Primary School, Manchester

WHAT DOES A MUM MEAN?

My mum is funny
And my mum is lovely.
My mum has good hair
And she is fair.
She cheers me up when I am blue
So I love you!

Mylo Thomas Li (6)

St Elizabeth's RC Primary School, Manchester

WHAT DOES A MUM MEAN?

My mum is kind,
She has the cleverest mind.

My mum cares for me,
She always shares with me.

My mum hates spiders,
She wears the best eyeliner.

My mum is the best mum ever!
I don't think I can get her better.

Lois

St Elizabeth's RC Primary School, Manchester

WHAT DOES A MUM MEAN?

My mum gives me lots of hugs,
She always carries lots of love.

My mum makes the best tea,
She always sets my love free.

My mum is really cool,
She always brings me presents when I get home from school.

My mum really is the best,
She is better than the rest!

Lily-Anne Ruby Toner
St Elizabeth's RC Primary School, Manchester

WHAT DOES A MUM MEAN?

I was in her tummy,
She is kind and funny.

My mum always tell me about sharing.
She always says, 'Sharing is caring'.

My mum has nice hair.
She is fair.

That's how much I love you.

Liv-Rose Hunt

St Elizabeth's RC Primary School, Manchester

WHAT DOES A MUM MEAN?

My mum is kind and funny.
She makes me rumble in my tummy.
My mum is the best
Of all the rest.
She always makes me a packed lunch.
My mum is strong and cool,
She always goes in the pool.
She is awesome and cool,
She used to go to school.
My mum is very kind
And she can find everything.
My mum is the best!

Freddie Edward Thorne (6)
St Elizabeth's RC Primary School, Manchester

WHAT DOES A MUM MEAN?

My mum is very cool,
She is always my crown jewel.

My mum's natural hair is brown,
I think she deserves a crown.

Mum loves our hugs,
She doesn't like many bugs.

My mum likes makeovers
But sometimes she does takeovers.

My mum hates spiders,
She wears the best eyeliner.

My mum is good at make-up,
She doesn't like to wake up.

Yuri Joyce
St Elizabeth's RC Primary School, Manchester

WHAT DOES A MUM MEAN?

My mum is funny,
She gives me food in my tummy.
My mum is very kind,
She always has others in mind.
I love my mum, what a star,
My love for you grows so far!

Amy Powell

St Elizabeth's RC Primary School, Manchester

WHAT DOES A MUM MEAN?

My mum is very brave and she is the best
And she has a rest
And she always keeps me filled up in my tummy.

My mummy is the best
And she makes me the best packed lunch ever.
She helps my baby brother from crying
And she knows when I'm lying.

Patrick Maher
St Elizabeth's RC Primary School, Manchester

My Mother

I love you Mum.
You are always there for me
When I'm sick
You never grumble or crumble.

I know you love me, Mum
You cook, clean
And read to me.
You are the best mum ever.

Asar Sesay
St John's Walworth CE Primary School, London

My Mum Is The Best

My mum is the best.
She is better than the rest.
She's like a tiger mum
I am the cub.
She cooks my food
On the hob.
My mum gives me love.
Even when I'm in the loft
She cares for me when I'm sad.
She cuddles and kisses me
When I am bad.

Henry Wallace

St John's Walworth CE Primary School, London

MARVELLOUS MUM

Mum, Mum
you are the best
under the sun.
I love you
for all you do.
Your eyes sparkle
when I look at you.
You are the best cook
without a book.
You help me clean
my room with the broom.
You are as beautiful as a dove.
You fill me with all your love.

Jayda Balogun
St John's Walworth CE Primary School, London

My Special Mother

Mother, Mother
I love you so much.
You make such good choices for me.
Mother, Mother
You give me love
No other can do.

Asier Dawit

St John's Walworth CE Primary School, London

HELPFUL MUM

She is helpful,
She is special,
She always cares for me,
Always crucial.

When I'm sick
She's there for me.
Beautiful as a Halloween trick.

I wish she would never grow old.
She's precious like a diamond.

Olivia Akua Twum

St John's Walworth CE Primary School, London

MY MUM IS THE BEST

I love my mummy very much,
She is very hardworking,
She helps me with my homework,
She loves me and looks after the cat and I well,
After my mum cooks dinner for me, she needs to relax,
At night, she reads to me,
She is very good at parking.

Benoit Kiesewetter

The Gower School, London

I Love You Mummy

I call my mum, Mummy,
My mummy helps me get dressed,
I love my mummy,
She gives me lots of cuddles and kisses,
My mummy makes me delicious food,
She lets me have some sleepovers at my friend's house
And she is really kind,
So on Sunday I will give her a very special breakfast.

Luella Facer

The Gower School, London

MY MUMMY IS SO FUNNY

I love my mummy so, so much,
But the problem is she is forgetful 24/7
But I love her,
My mummy is funny,
I love her so much,
She helps me get dressed,
She gives me cuddles,
I love Mummy.

Eliza Horgan

The Gower School, London

My Mum Is The Most Beautiful

I love my mum,
She is beautiful,
She gives me cuddles,
She gets me big toys,
She loves me more but I love her more.

Daniyal Gilkar

The Gower School, London

YES I DO LOVE MY MUMMY

I love my mummy, yes I do,
She is nice and amazing too,
She cares about me,
She is very sweet,
She is clever,
She is cuddly
And makes me feel unique.

Adria DeHart

The Gower School, London

MY MUMMY CARES FOR ME

I love my mummy,
She plays with me.
She cooks my dinner,
She brings me to nice places.
She helps me when I feel grumpy.
She prints out my photos
And puts me to bed and cuddles me.

Anna Bonaria Mameli

The Gower School, London

I Love My Mummy

I love my mummy so much,
She is a really nice girl.
She is nice at all times,
She is my favourite person.
She is nice to me.
My mummy loves me so much,
But there is one thing.
She thinks she loves me more,
But I actually love her more than she does.

Iyla Ranawat
The Gower School, London

My Mummy Loves Me So Much

My mum is kind, my mum is fun,
My mum is funny; she makes me laugh.
She makes me happy because she is very caring.
My mum's favourite colour is green
And my mum likes music.
She likes cooking food,
My favourite is chicken and pasta.
My mum is really protective.
When a stranger asked if I wanted a sweetie
My mum said no!
You are the best Mum ever.

Pietro Rizzo Faro

The Gower School, London

MOTHER'S DAY IS THE BEST

M other's Day is lovely, Mother's Day is the best

O ther days are fine

T ogether we make a team

H ide I might but you will always find me out. Love will
never

E nd

R umours might break your heart but you will always
recover

S ometimes you are happy and sometimes you are sad but
that will never stop your love. You always like things neat
and sometimes you're

D istressed

A t most times you are happy

Y ou always love sushi because it is very yummy.

Abi Cantor

The Gower School, London

MY MUMMY IS SO KIND

I love Mummy because she is very kind,
She is a good cook and she makes yummy food,
We chat together and it makes me feel happy,
Mummy is creative and makes things with me,
She is always nice and gives me big hugs,
Me and Mum go out together,
I love my mummy.

Luke Tomlinson

The Gower School, London

MY MUMMY IS THE BEST!

M ummy is the best
Y ummy food she cooks for us

M ummy helps me with everything (well, nearly everything)
U sually she is very funny
M ummy helps me with a lot
M ummy makes me feel very safe
Y esterday my mummy helped me when I felt sad

I love you, Mummy
S he loves me and my daddy a lot

T ogether we read books
H ugs we give to each other
E nding the book, we laugh out loud together

B est of all my mummy is the best
E very day we laugh out loud
S tanding we do art together
T alking and chatting all day long.

Sophie Basile

The Gower School, London

My Mummy Makes Me Laugh

Mummy is so good,
She cooks my favourite meal,
Pizza!
She cares about me
And she helps me with my homework.
She keeps me safe and makes me laugh.
Rufus and I love her.
We are too busy hugging her to do anything else.

Jesper Guise
The Gower School, London

MOTHERS ARE KIND

M others are kind
O n and in their mind
T ogether and apart
H over in a heart
E very mother's great
R unning and always late
S winging around and

D ancing round
A nd lovely mothers
Y ummy others.

Lia Matos Wunderlich

The Gower School, London

MY MUMMY IS WONDERFUL

My mummy is wonderful and special
Because she takes me to school.
Mummy is very kind and helpful.
We are always leaping.
She loves me very much
And we love her too.

Phoebe Swift

The Notley Green Primary School, Braintree

LOVE MUM

My mummy loves us,
We love her back.
When she takes us out
We really, really like it.
She is the best mummy in the world!

Noah O'Sullivan

The Notley Green Primary School, Braintree

MY SUPER MUM

Super Mum is super sweet.
Super Mum is super neat.
Super Mum is super cool.
Super Mum plays with me all day
And that's not all.
Super Mum colours with me
And talks with me which is lots of fun.
Super Mum is Number One.

Olivia Christy

The Notley Green Primary School, Braintree

MY SUPER MUM

When I am sad she makes me happy
and full of joy.
She calls me her little monster but really,
I am her precious boy.
She makes all my food and cleans all my clothes,
Keeps me from the cold and kisses my nose.
She makes me laugh with tickles and funny faces,
But there to help me with my shoe laces.
She explains things I don't understand
By sitting me down and holding my hand.
She tells me she loves me each and every day
And I am special in every way.
She reads me a bedtime story
and tucks me in at night
And always turns on my bedroom light.
She is always happy but sometimes gets cross,
She is my super mum, I call her *the boss!*

Tommy Allport

The Notley Green Primary School, Braintree

ETERNAL LOVE

You taught me the right from the wrong.
You sat up with me through the nights so long,
On the days when I was sick and bad.
Today, I just want to tell you, Mother
It is only you who understands.
I love you so much.
Happy Mother's Day to you!
Love your beautiful daughter, Chloe!

Chloe Bernard

The Notley Green Primary School, Braintree

MY NAN

My nan is wonderful,
It is totally true.
We bond in the same way
Just like me and you.

I come to her in school holidays,
On weekends too.
I love it with her so much,
But that is my view.

She knits me clothes
And buys me bows.
She will hold my hamster
And stroke and pamper.

We play board games
And never blame
The other person for cheating.
We ride bikes
And go on hikes.
Every step is loving.

The reason she is wonderful
Is because of who she is.
Her twinkling eyes and loving smile
But I have a tricky quiz.
How is she so incredible?
It is making my mind whiz!

I love my nan,
Extremely so.
She is the best nan in the world,

But just so she knows.
I love my amazing nan,
I am her number one fan.

Amelie Field
The Notley Green Primary School, Braintree

BEST MUM!

Our mum is like a crazy person having fun,
Loud when she shouts like a bongo drum,
She sings very badly but she thinks she's great
And she makes us do hugs even if we're late,
Mostly she's cool and huggy and fun
And that's the reason we love our mum.

George Maximus Turner & Leo Turner

The Notley Green Primary School, Braintree

I LOVE MY MUMMY A TON

My mummy is the best mum,
She always gives me treats,
Especially after she cooks a super-duper feast.

She lets me on the PlayStation
And she takes me football training,
Even when it is cold outside
And sometimes when it's raining.

She always gives me kisses
And huggles before I go to bed
And if I have been really good
I get to watch a film in bed.

She lets me play in the garden
If it's nice and sunny,
These are just a few things
I love about my mummy.

Jackson Harry Blake Woodward

The Notley Green Primary School, Braintree

ALL ABOUT MY MUM

From screams to cries,
Walking to running
You helped me through these times.
I feel lost without you
You make my heart full
As we catch each other's eyes.

Mum,
You are kind and helpful
And respectful to all.
You make me smile
Big or small.

My mum is great;
She's sweet as she can be.
When I need some help I know
Mum will be there for me.

When I get older
I know I will be
Kind and loving as you are to me.

Soon I'll leave home
Start my own beginning
Tears rolling down my face
But all I need to know
Is that Mum is by my side
Looking out for me
Every step of the way.

Maisie Speller (11)

The Notley Green Primary School, Braintree

FOR MY MUM

My mum is always there for me when
I need her the most,
She makes me laugh when I am sad
And she is not the kind
Who will nag when you are bad.

She is a person who is kind and gentle,
But on the rare occasions she can be a bit mental,
I love her the way she is
And there is nothing I would change about her,
When I look at her I see a brave, strong-minded girl
And now I know her she is as soft as a pearl.

My mum is a bouquet of flowers,
Always bringing joy and happiness to the world
She is the person I am always curled up with.

She is always near me with an open heart
And she is like a star,
I can't always see her but I know she is there
And I will love her with all my heart and more,
Because my mother is the best I could ever hope for!

Ruby Paris Filmer

The Notley Green Primary School, Braintree

MUMMY

We go on hikes,
We love our bikes,
We snuggle together,
I wish we could forever.
We love playing cards
And gazing at stars.
We have a bond so strong,
It will never break.
We love our time baking cakes,
You tell me you love me every day.
I'm content in every way!

Tahlia Haylock

The Notley Green Primary School, Braintree

MY WONDERFUL MUM

You are the sunlight in my day,
You are the moon I see far away,
You are the tree I leap upon,
You are the one that makes troubles be gone,
My wonderful mum.

Your hair blows in the wind,
You make my heart unpinned,
Your bracelet tingles when you hold my hand,
You are amazingly grand,
My wonderful mum.

She looks nothing like a dove,
She is the only one I love.

Amy Parker

The Notley Green Primary School, Braintree

MY MUMMY

My mummy cares for me every day,
She helps me when I need it most.
If I need advice or just need some love.
We both like running across the fields
In summer full of daisies hand in hand
With our summer dresses swaying in the cool wind.
She cooks me dinner which is lovely.
I couldn't thank Mummy enough.
Thank you, Mummy.

Daisi Jane Archer

The Notley Green Primary School, Braintree

MUMMY AND ME

Best mummy in the world,
When I am sad, Mummy makes me feel fab.
My mummy has a big, pure heart made from gold,
She gives me big bear hugs.

Maddie Knight (7)

The Notley Green Primary School, Braintree

MY MUM

My mum would do anything for me,
My mum would eat a bumblebee!
My mum is the best there can be,
My mum is always there for me.
She would always smile and understand mistakes.
She hasn't tried but I bet she can make cakes.
My mum is as kind as can be.
My mum always loves me.
My mum would spend all her money.
My mum would do it to save me.
I love my mum for all there can be.
I love spending time with her, just her and me.

Dexter Draper

The Notley Green Primary School, Braintree

MY MUM IS...

My mummy is so generous.
She helps me night and day.
I will always love your happy smile.
Mummy, you're the best one by a mile.
You smell like roses and daffodils.
Mummy, I love you so, so, so much.

Amelia Rose Green

Victoria College Preparatory School, Belfast

MY MUM IS...

My mum is an amazing dog walker.
She helps me with my homework.
You always make me lovely dinners and lunches.
You are always thoughtful and kind to me.
At bedtime you tuck me into my bed.
I love you lots and lots and lots Mummy.

Grace Anna Nelson

Victoria College Preparatory School, Belfast

MY MUM IS...

My mummy loves me.
She gives me big hugs.
She is funny.
She is kind.
She is caring.
My mummy is very pretty.
She tells the truth.
She is fun.
She is happy.
She is the best
Mummy in the world!

Maria Garcia Kehoe (7)
Victoria College Preparatory School, Belfast

MY MUM IS...

My mum is...
Beautiful, blonde and lovely.
My mummy is nice and kind,
Caring and smart,
Amazing and giving,
Thoughtful and wonderful,
Super and good, lovely and funny.
My mummy is pretty and great.
Leader of me, silly and great,
I love her to the moon and back!

Ella Gordon (7)

Victoria College Preparatory School, Belfast

My Mum Is...

Dear Mummy...
You are smart, pretty and true,
I will never leave you
'Cause I am the very last.
I love you Mummy from top to bottom
'Cause you are my mummy!

Freya Clementine Birney

Victoria College Preparatory School, Belfast

My Mum Is...

My mummy is prettier than a butterfly.
She makes me giggle with joy.
When I see her dangly earrings shining in my eyes,
I wish they were mine.
She truly loves me.
My mummy is confident.
She's really kind, maybe she's kinder than Santa?
She's definitely not strict, not even a bit.

Paige Somorin (7)

Victoria College Preparatory School, Belfast

UNTITLED

Super Mum, you're the best ,
You are better than the rest.
With you with me I'm truly blessed,
You even helped me pass my test!

You give me guidance when I ask,
You always fulfil every task.
You bought me a new football face-mask,
You even filled up my new flask!

You definitely are a rising star,
You're not perfect but you're not far.
Mother's day - 26th of March,
Which is why we're gathering where we are.

I love you Mum,
The flowers have already uncurled.
I think you're the best,
As good as the world!
Super Mum!

Dylan Burke

Whiteknights Primary School, Reading

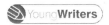

SUPER MUM

Super Mum, super Mum, super Mum
Her cooking is the best
Super mum, super mum
She never has a rest
She cooks and cleans and washes too
At home she never stops
And when the cleaning's finished she runs off to the shops
In getting us all ready she really goes berserk
And all of this she has to do before she goes to work
Super mum, super mum
She must have superpowers
'Cause every day she seems to fit no less than 50 hours
She really is a wonder
This fact is oh so true
But what is most important,
Mum, is how much we love you.

Freya Curtis

Whiteknights Primary School, Reading

AMAZING MUMS

My mum is amazing,
Always by my side,
She's always there when I need help,
She helped me when I cried.

My mum is a pretty pearl,
She'll always shine right through,
Mum is always helping,
She's always lovely too.

I'll always love you Mum,
She's always up to the test,
I'll never forget you,
Mum, you're the best!

Hadiyah Golaup (8)

Whiteknights Primary School, Reading

THE DREAM MUM

In a dream in the past
It went so fast, a dream in the past
I dreamed of a mum, who loved bubble gum

We would play games, and think of nicknames
She would do the washing up, including my cup
My blanket so dirty,
Reminds me of Birty,

O golly,
It looks like Aunt Holly,
Mum's sister,
Mum says she's a blister,

Covering me in kisses,
Fulfilling my wishes
Washing the dishes
I love my mum, she loves me too
She's always fun, I love her puns, my mum.

Peace Motunrayo Bamidele
Whiteknights Primary School, Reading

Super Mummy

Mum would be a mumbly but you
Clean, iron and give us a hug
When I was a baby you gave me hugs like you still do
You are the best mummy because you give me good
presents
I do not know what I will do without you
You are so special
You are special because you have a special belly
You make the best dinners, and you are the very best mum,
So that's why I do my homework,
And read with you because I am the best daughter ever.

Lily-Mae (10)
Whiteknights Primary School, Reading

SUPER MUM

Super Mum
Better than the rest
My life is amazing because of you
Your cooking is the best
You never have a rest
You always do the dishes
You always grant my wishes
She always gives me kisses
Mum, you're so pure and true
I think about you all the time
I love you.

Makiya Roberts
Whiteknights Primary School, Reading

Young Writers
Information

We hope you have enjoyed reading this book – and
that you will continue to in the coming years.

If you're a young writer who enjoys reading and creative
writing, or the parent of an enthusiastic poet or story writer,
do visit our website www.youngwriters.co.uk. Here you will
find free competitions, workshops and games, as well as
recommended reads, a poetry glossary and our blog.

If you would like to order further copies of this book, or any of
our other titles give us a call or visit www.youngwriters.co.uk.

Young Writers
Remus House
Coltsfoot Drive
Peterborough
PE2 9BF

(01733) 890066
info@youngwriters.co.uk